Jacob Hoke Beidler

Lincoln; or, the Prime Hero of the Nineteenth Century

Jacob Hoke Beidler

Lincoln; or, the Prime Hero of the Nineteenth Century

ISBN/EAN: 9783337191146

Printed in Europe, USA, Canada, Australia, Japan

Cover: Foto ©ninafisch / pixelio.de

More available books at **www.hansebooks.com**

LINCOLN

OR THE

Prime Hero of the Nineteenth Century

❧

By J. H. Beidler

❧

PUBLISHED BY GRACIA BEIDLER & CO.
CHICAGO, ILL.
1896

PREAMBLE.

No ancient rule or style-constructing lines
Diverting author from his own designs,
Who sought the trail the lad and Hero did,
Whose mind was dauntless, and no fault was hid,
Imbuing author thus, inspiring heart
To build in freedom, if not framed in art;
The terse and rugged was his Hero's style,
As midst the rumbling thunders he would smile,
Love's tenderness and truth made Lincoln strong
To live, to labor, rectifying wrong.

SYLLABUS.

HERE thirteen thousand syllables of sound,
Of breathing life in giving facts, are found ;
From helpless babe to youth, from lad to age
And empty hands, to power and tragic stage,
The grandeur of his force, and how it grew
Until it compassed what was then in view ;
His human efforts built with proper plan
To dignify the highest place of man,
With upright heart, and fertile brain of toil,
And power within himself, as seed in soil.

PREFATORY.

SHALL I regret the authorship of this
    The many days and nights of mental toil,
As labor mingled with its fleeting bliss,
    Whilst mixing iridescence with the oil?
Shall I regret I ever knew the man,
    Whose living presence studied with an aim,
As hidden embers winds began to fan,
    Igniting like volcano into flame?

I heard him speak, accenting special word —
    Observing mind as he declaimed for hours,
With thorny wit his jury often stirred,
    Then striking blows with great forensic powers.
Shall I regret I lived within his years,
    Partaking of his times with mighty men?
The thinking era, full of love and tears, —
    A thousand years were crystalized in ten.

He came unconscious to parental care,
　Whose mind burst open full as rose on thorn,
Spontaneous evidence made him aware
　That great inherent force in him was born.
With ax and book, no day of life to waste,
　Whose mental energies increase desires,
In eagerness developed solid taste —
　That thoughts and soul, with purposes inspires.

All perfect children in their being hold
　A spark of God's divinity in trust,
For human knowledge kindly to unfold,
　And spirit power with intellect adjust.
The more divinity, the purer child,
　Exhibited by modesty, so much
That growing manhood could not be defiled ;
　Was Lincoln not the evidence of such ?

Park Beidler,   BEIDLER.
　　　　July 4, 1896.

PROLOGUE.

I OFTEN gazed on his athletic form,
As if I stood before approaching storm ;
I felt a hidden force was brewing there,
To culminate would energize despair.
His face an outline map, distinct in shape,
And one the student's eye could not escape.
Each line marked vastness, tho' in strange reserve,
As strength and wonder formed the line of curve,
His soul and intellect expansion sought —
Unfettered spirit, shackles ever fought.

Corroding avarice dishonors bring,
The stingy dollar had to him no ring.
He looked through telescope of largest lens
To see beginning, and where purpose ends.
The planets intonated songs to him —
Sad Luna, queen of eve, his solace hymn ;
The wind, his song of nature's lullaby,
And storm, his oratorio of sky ;
The wildest nature charmed the searching man,
And no phenomenon he did not scan.

NATIVITY.

Was he the child of freedom destiny had shaped
Within the womb of purity, feebleness escaped,
Whose mother's blood, Teutonic, pure and undefiled,
Through Anglo-Saxon father came the rugged child?
What drafts of inspiration mother did enjoy,
In giving proud Kentucky enigmatic boy,
With all climatic forces, food and healthy air,
The greater force prenatal, — mother's larger share.

That she was overshadowed heaven better knows,
That he was born for purpose country's record shows.
How ultra complicated; simple tho' the truth,
The helpless babe of love developed into youth ; —
For boy of tangled hair becomes the ruling force,
And destinies of nations tremble at his course.
The birth of Lincoln fixed the epoch of the age,
And most heroic actor on the tragic stage.

Unheralded he came with his reliant power,
To grow in silent culture till the promised hour,
Then rise above horizon, vulcan-like he grows,
To forge new sentiments by his resistless blows.
He shaped his span of time with purposes to fit,
With wisdom more elastic than didactic wit;
He conquered peace with war, the nation's foremost son;
And fell in tragic fame, when victory was won.

LINCOLN'S OPEN-ACRE HOME.

THE climbing rose around this cabin bloomed,
And Open-Acre's solitude perfumed ;
Its tendrils clasp the logs with sacred cling,
And lending pleasure to each living thing.
Here child and mother hours in silence spent,
Enduing each with its inspiring scent.

THE WAY.

FROM manger to the sacrificial cross,
What holy way He trod, no second's loss,
From conquest unto victory.   His march
The way prepared 'neath firmamental arch.

THE ROAD.

AGAIN behold! Where solitude repines
And virtue reigns, whilst Heaven still designs,
In deep seclusion rocked a blessed babe;
Prophetic faith of love dictated Abe.
What rugged road he trod to marble flights,
A sacrifice of life to human rights.

LINCOLN'S CABIN HOME.

Dear hearth of childhood, sacred still that home,
With clay-built chimney ventilating dome ;
Thy fire ignited torch with lurid blaze
To light my path that leads to broader ways.

LINCOLN'S SPRINGFIELD HOME.

This home of manhood now inspiring life
With ties of love in children, mother, wife ;
Undying embers changeless glow the same,
That lit ambition's torch to modest flame.

LINCOLN AT THE WHITE HOUSE.

As chosen magistrate its duties I assume,
Midst overspreading clouds, and deep, foreboding gloom ;
To unify in peace becomes my sacred task.
Will heaven grant us that for which I humbly ask?
May God turn back the dark approaching storm of woe,
And wisdom grant to all, and mercy still bestow,
And save the daring father and intrepid son ;
In union must be peace, disunion offers none.

LINCOLN'S MIDNIGHT PRAYER.

JUST AFTER THE BATTLE OF BULL RUN.

"Thou God who heard a Solomon at night,
When praying for true wisdom and for light,
Hear me! I cannot lead this people so,
I cannot guide affairs of nation, No!
Without Thy help. I'm sinful, poor, and weak,
Thy holy wisdom I in mercy seek,
O God! who didst hear Solomon, and gave
Him wisdom, hear me; and the Nation save."

THE FATAL NIGHT.

THAT fatal eve lit star-bespangled skies —
A cloud obscured a star from Lincoln's eyes,
Remarking, "Night, let not a star be hid.
Thy splendor's infinite, what shall forbid?
Whose eyes could tire, as twinkling height declares
The majesty and power each planet shares;
That changes darkness into stellar light —
Where distant space enjoys creative might?
This night I'll cherish heaven's luring charms,
With peace on earth, and hushed the rattling arms."

His soul ecstatic, contemplating peace,
He saw the fruits of war at once increase;
Triumphant army welcomed had returned.
The gratitude of peace on altar burned,
And Lincoln's palm had grasped the soldier hand;
The capital aflame as they disband,
As North rejoiced, the South could do no less,
Decree of right was honored, peace to bless.
The fatal hour approached, the moment came,
Our Hero fell from our last foeman's aim!

LINCOLN'S HEROIC ADDRESS

BEFORE

THE CELESTIAL PORTALS.

Apostolic Servant :

A flying messenger of sudden death
Or painless shock, divorcing life of breath,
Has placed me by those portals I behold ;
The facts, by your permission, shall unfold,
As humble servant cheerfully I wait,
Before the majesty of heaven's gate ;
But yesterday I stood in whirling time,
I think, the public subject of a crime ;
Yet conscious, and with forcible surprise,
Identity in transit realize.

Four score and seven years ago, our sires
Brought forth a nation of their own desires,
Of equal states of free and slave in part,
A perfect union.   Formed by brain and heart.
A nation "of the people" and the states.
Conceived in liberty and wise debates,
And "by the people" freedom to secure,
And "for the people" ever to endure,
"Not perish from the earth," as Greece and Rome,
"As government" protecting every home.

Bright sun of freedom, long eclipsed in part,
Refused full glow of light to son of mart.
One pigment cell to line of human kin,
Denied them freedom, 'derm however thin.
Men saw pigmented Venus, blushing fresh,
Upon the owner's block, and sold as flesh.
I watched and trembled, thinking of my God,
Extending mercy and withholding rod,
But rights of man are heritage of brave,
Servility foul heritage of slave.

Had I electric tongue and lips of steel,
My ignified conclusions would reveal.
But let me speak as I have ne'er before,
Since called to serve my people, to restore
A fragmentary nation to a whole —
With sentiments divided to control ;
My life was as a ray, 'mong rising beams,
Commingled with horizon's morning gleams.
One single ray may light in early hour,
Some crooked path with unexpected power.

My words of peace the cannon quickly hushed,
In mockery my sentiments were crushed,
A nation full of will, sublime in power,
Had plucked me as from limb in fruitful bower ;
Not ripe, as many others on the tree,
I grew on northern branch, by slow degree ;
Not season-painted beauty, tint of east,
The morning sun had flavored for a feast ;
My growth partook of twig, and soil of clay,
And all climatic forces of each day.

I speak in parable, as highest truth.
As of my own maturity and youth,
I am God's being, not deceptive ghost,
To higher rise than time's ethereal coast ;
I was not raised 'a Nero, cruel czar,
But faithful student at my country's bar.
The people's choice for magistrate as one
To catch the fiery darts whom others shun,
And heal the angry wounds already made,
While lending life of strength to country's aid.

Impetuosity, climatic bred,
Secession's turbulence ambition fed ;
Men's long environments established law
No culpability in bondsman saw,
From sire to son, from bride to husband came,
Inheritance of slaves through legal claim ;
Like Ananias' land, the slave was sold,
Oft given church, converted into gold ;
The pious slave served man and God in fact
While deacon vigil kept o'er every act.

Servility had incubated rage,
With sword and arm to strike, at given stage,
Spasmodic spirits grew eccentric, wild,
The Constitution in their wrath reviled,
Defying power ordained by peace and war,
Distorting truth that virtue must abhor ;
State prejudices grew as sparks to flame,
While loyal Southerners their madness blame,
Fire-eaters and philosophers debate,
As sister States unsheathed the sword of fate.

Our nation had a grand, exalted birth,
And therefore "shall not perish from the earth."
Dark pigment cell a mighty power concealed,
Mulatto with Caucasian blood revealed —
Preponderance increased no right or claim —
The master held all rights, in moral shame ;
The wrongs of man to man compounded hate,
And no relief from heaven, or of State.
The moans and groans, the whip and block of mart —
Combustibles igniting human heart.

On quiv'ring scale the poise of war was hung,
Two flags on native soil, to breezes flung,
Exaggeration's secessional shuttle drove,
And web of conflict in excitement wove,
Until the land, from rivers to the sea,
The threatened battle-ground between the free ;
Great brains and hearts, devoted to each cause,
Then rushed to arms without dissenting pause ;
The force of war's upheaval moved each one,
Conviction taking sides, from sire to son.

The sword was not the weapon of my choice,
For reason passionless was heaven's voice.
But Southern chivalry first urged the powers,
For destiny to crush exotic flowers ;
They casting problems in disunion molds,
We twining olive-branch in starry folds,
The constellation peaceable would save ;
Its failure, pinioned harbinger of slave,
Seceding stars in darkness never set,
Nor struggle dimmed a ray with one regret.

Now dire transition peace at once expels ;
Fort guns were turned on ships, with shot and shells,
Which overt act inaugurated war,
Provoking North to its dilating core.
Cyclonic like, sons whirled to either side,
Two armies soon equipped, of youthful pride ;
On fields for gory deeds, in battle met,
Determined foes for conquest anxious fret,
Untarnished sword unsheathed for blood and death,
While peace neutrality was catching breath.

The hearts of Christians felt the trial of woe
The church and state for decades helped to grow
Yet vying with each other in the dare,　＇
In battle fought without a panic scare ;
No person'l hatred had evolved the war,
All thought they knew what each was serving for,
Like eagles hatched in one parental nest
Of equal courage, on their valor rest,
And none but Heaven's power could call a halt —
Imperturbation heated to revolt.

State capitals became the camping-grounds,
And every wind full laden, hostile sounds,
Defenses built from coasts to hills and streams,
As bayonet by corps in battle gleams ;
Aggressive war finds forts and trenches filled
With native blood and restless heroes killed ·
Two million men engaged in battle fray,
And crowded hospitals of Blue and Gray,
With prisons full, and land of open graves
To welcome soldiers ; mariners the waves.

Defeat and victory, they each sustain,
As corps on corps repulsed to form again,
Both arms infatuated with success,
Attack with reinforcement, forward press;
From horse to horse their sabers interchange,
While great columbiads swept at distant range;
When thousands fell where slaves for ages trod,
All wounded prayed to one eternal God;
Devoted to their cause of section 'l strife,
And sealed devotion with their ebbing life.

Hot battles fought in all the Southern States,
And death seemed swinging open holy gates,
For thousands fled with sunsets flushing red,
On whose fair border I now humbly tread;
Defeat and victory did each inspire;
From every section came the telling wire,
Intensifying minutes with the news.
War scenes occurred whatever place we choose,
'T was war at home, in church, in prayer, in song,
The talk of war was heard from every tongue.

Perplexing and mysterious force of war
Was felt to ebb and flow from coast to shore ·
The change of politics rebuked a halt,
And captious Mars withdrew in cloudy vault;
As doubt eclipsed bright visions with delays,
Cold, misanthropic minds reject God's ways;
In midst of nation'l gravity I stood,
To halt, inglorious; action, Freedomhood!
God's proclamation then to breezes hurled,
And stars and stripes to human rights unfurled.

Then followed victories, from forts to fleets,
As "Monitor" the "Merrimac" defeats.
While gulf and rivers ironclads patrol,
The world our navy victories extol,
Proud cities devastated 'neath our arms,
Plantation too, as cotton fields and farms,
The cry of war supplanting household joy,
While taxing art for engines to destroy;
The trail of conflict drenched in crimson woe
As devastation wrought war's overthrow.

What unsurpassing glory war revealed !
Brave generosity to heart appealed,
Capitulation came to sheathe the sword
In winding-sheet, "Lost Cause" to peace restored.
The brave surrender to the brave in arms,
Transmuting gore to antidotal charms,
The cry "To arms," was changed to whisp'ring peace,
As corps disperse, the strides for home increase,
With freedom's possibilities ajar,
To open swing, without a lock or bar.

Three long, disastrous years of war and gore,
With moral tension, strongest fiber tore.
All crops neglected, life and treasure lost,
And happy hearths destroyed at bitter cost ;
Then reconciliation ; peace restored,
And hostile flag was furled, and sheathed the sword.
The songs of peace were sung by soldiers' voice,
One common country, all in love rejoice ;
With crown of liberty on every head,
And green the graves of all the noble dead.

Relieved by Providence, without appeal,
As chief of nation, nothing to conceal,
Rejoicing, for my country's peace I love;
I'm thankful to my God that I'm above.
"With charity for all," I plead for each,
His benediction ask, and do beseech;
For we were brothers, but not understood,
But now the problem's solved for highest good;
No life was given Heaven will not bless,
In solemn judgment I do here profess.

Our conflict raised my estimate of men,
Augmenting faith in righteous sword and pen;
Our nation great, of chivalry and pluck,
The highest attitude of purpose struck;
To struggle for their rights, with heart and hand,
And seeing right from their peculiar stand,
As your unselfish stroke when holding sword,
Who cut the ear, the Master's touch restored.
What grand display of love in each we see,
Who died for what he thought was God's decree!

LINCOLN'S ADDRESS.

He who doth give his life for noble cause,
Enshrines himself in highest moral laws ;
Such men crave naught but truth while loving right
Are ever rising upward in their flight ;
No falt 'ring second chills their honest soul,
Nor slow regret their purposes control ;
They die for love of right to better all,
Whose purpose flaming gulf cannot appal,
Their souls seem fortified with special grace ;
Where duty calls, they find their chosen place.

In dawn's dim distance utterance became
The power of language, as caloric flame ;
Elastic Anglo-Saxon, later born,
Our hearths and forums learnedly adorn ;
Selecting signs and Greek and Roman words,
Phenician sounds from hieroglyphic birds,
Our English must be clear to you, tho' young,
Your scope of knowledge takes in every tongue ;
Words are but laden breath of vocal sound,
Yet grave and simple as they are profound.

No royal despot breathes our native air
Nor crown conflicts with governmental care.
Had Christ been born on freedom's blessed land,
Where people rule, and legal votes command,
No hand had nailed Him to Historic Tree,
By strange ecclesiastical decree;
Where thoughts are free as liberty on wings,
All blessing to the people equal brings,
The child of indigence, or Heaven's Son,
Bright stars and stripes enfold the weakest one.

The country, standing monument of right,
As Jesus taught before He took His flight,
Who elevated man to noble sphere,
Self-government approved is conscious clear;
None have the right of other's blood and sweat,
Without the recompense their toils beget;
Equality of Gentile and the Jew,
You taught so eloquently, must be true;
I stood upon the bridge's extending span,
To represent equality of man.

That bridge was more than sordid human skill ;
Our fathers were the instruments of will,
Who built it strong on which I firmly stood,
With faith and trust in vitalizing good ;
That arch of liberty a union spans,
Unbroken structure, wisdom's latest plans ;
The weight of millions time shall never break,
That arch of strength what human efforts shake ?
It stands the glory of a struggling past,
Sustaining weight as limitless as vast.

My cabinet were men at once renowned,
Nor firmer counsel in the nation found.
Philosophers and statesmen my support,
Exalted jurists that composed the court.
Distinguished heroes, incarnated white,
As academic scholars taught to fight ;
While sovereign people to my counsel clung,
As true as bees, disloyal apis stung.
Each sacrificed without a murm'ring pause,
Upon the altar of their country's cause.

The cross, with solemn purpose, light, and power,
Shed glory on the cause's triumphant hour.
The love of patriot partook of force, ·
Evolving from the purest, noblest source,
Which justified the work of crimson flow,
With proffered charity at every blow ;
The Union crystalized without a flaw,
And Constitution saved as highest law,
" Unalienable rights " for all secured,
And constellated stars their light assured.

I held the sword of conflict at command,
One foot on waves, the other on the land ;
Where'er the flag was kissed by heaven's breeze,
Its majesty 's upheld on land or seas ;
As victories had vindicated cause,
Beneficent results acclaim applause.
Revenge I knew not, pity sought control,
While equity and mercy poised my soul ;
Responsibility I felt, of state,
As tragic force, accumulative weight.

War-anguish mothers felt were pangs too keen
When mingled tears and kiss in parting seen ;
The sobbing child and melancholy lass,
Soul-painted pictures still through mem'ry pass.
My pen was ever ready life to save,
And even guilty spies a pardon gave ;
How oft my prayers have winged to God to learn
Where mercy ends, and justice must return ;
My solemn duty was to do my part,
No dregs are in my cup, or sting in heart.

I oft have tasted glorified reward,
Men justifying acts with one accord,
I tried with bloodless measures to adjust
Which fell as spray upon the desert dust,
To see the blackest moment flash emit
Abyss of darkness unexpected lit.
Red stars in azure in an instant hide
Yet men of honest souls in truth abide
And man of Christlike spirit wrong defy
With sword of death in gore as Christian die.

Our person'l conflict desolation's womb,
Tho' soon became mutation's open tomb,
To which was doomed what freedom had denied,
As Pharaoh's host was plunged beneath the tide ;
For Moses and Elias seemed on earth,
With heaven's power of sanctifying worth,
And lending light as moon and stars and sun,
Bright rays of liberty for every one
With pigments black as spiral hair on head,
Or forest athlete, with his pigments red.

True liberty of conscience lends delight,
As liberty of person stands for right ;
All intellect with freedom must expand —
Developed mind prepares the skilful hand ;
As great constructive age enhanced the hour,
Creative brains become the motive power ;
Our engines rival wings and hoofs, to run,
Chronometer ticks time with earth and sun ;
Our telescope wipes distance from the eyes,
And chemistry lights occults with surprise.

To me the stars seemed scintillating gold,
As firmament of night would things unfold,
And rising sun augmented beams to shine
From blue meridian with power divine ;
Each silent ray sent forth a vital power,
With earnest purpose soothing anxious hour,
Which gave me strength in sadness, even might,
With comfort to my soul, the cause was right ;
Upon my country's altar all was placed,
With my command no life was spent as waste.

Hence nation'l liberty with knowledge grows,
As mind develops heart, it overflows ;
The cross shines brighter, when it 's understood,
To learn God's chastisements were serving good ;
The blood-fed soil shall corn and cotton yield,
And happy homes of freedom dot the field ;
To ocean's breath hydraulic force of wave
Shall carry trade, and wharfs of commerce lave ;
A continental union ocean bound
Shall nurture liberty wherever found.

The depths of past and solemn presence tell
That not a sparrow falls, nor soldier fell
But purpose filled, however deeply veiled,
While negative of right has always failed.
Whatever part the majesty of place
Conferred on me, with heaven's goodly grace,
I ventured all my being, hope, and force,
And history may justify my course ;
I ask no honor, truth for me shall care,
If my short presence served my people there.

My exit was as calm as voyage clear,
Exhilarating ecstasy to cheer.
Without exertion, power I think divine,
Has urged my passage, pregnant with design ;
I am myself, and tangibly I vow ;
Please solve the problem of my presence now ;
Those hingeless portals Vulcan could not forge,
Bright, swinging mountains over sapphire gorge,
Beyond, what raptured intellectu'l joy
Where souls can highest faculties employ !

My visions in the past, however true,
Are here eclipsed with forces startling, new ;
Time's theories blooming on the tree, or shoot,
Are here fruition, knowledge's ripened fruit ;
Past mental glimmers, now refulgent light,
And wings of doubt deprived of further flight.
Philosophy of Christ doth constant shine,
Emphatic truth embellished with divine,
Time's purifying agony of heart,
Prepares for such sublimity in part.

New glimpse of spirit light oft reason lit,
Then peals of moral thunder followed it.
And some unknown, occult, ignited soul,
As laden seconds passed beyond control ;
My mind partook of all that I now see,
Then passing gleams ; here all intensity.
Could brave agnostic friends see what I do,
Their feeble minds might feed on something new ;
The rising glory of eternal light,
Where finite thought with infinite unite.

The flames and ashes of explosive past,
Were fanned and driven by aggressive blast ;
Time's weight of ignorance in servile march,
Too ponderous for freedom's moral arch ;
But opulence and indolence remain,
That forged the frow, to rive us into twain ;
None but a God who end and purpose knew
Could stop opposing power of Gray and Blue ;
I come as pleading harbinger of love
To plead the rights of man in courts above.

Humanity has claims which God allows,
When man to Fatherhood in wisdom bows ;
To breathe divinity as vital air,
But life's responsibility must share.
The flag of peace is flag of rightful war,
A living fact, without disjunctive "or,"
Philosophy and duty filled the ranks
When lottery of life dispensed no blanks.
Tho' coward's impulse with ambition's aim,
Ignited spontaneity to flame.

Apostle thou ; denied our Master thrice,
At tearful cost and penitential price ;   [we learned ;
"Thou thought'st thou would'st not, but thou didst,"
Humanity how frail when life 's concerned !
But frailty must be ours; my faith held out
And right prevailed, defeating sheltered doubt ;
Emancipation's work doth promise well,
Without a clank, four million shackles fell.
Yes ! liberty has spread new pinions wide,
And God has granted what man long denied.

Your tribulations conquered all your foes,
Those portal keys you hold through martyr's woes ;
No fagot pyre nor cross deterred thy step,
In justice drew the sword, in sorrow wept ;
You heard the Master's words on mount and sea,
You learned of Him through mysteries to see,
Whose wisdom echoes still throughout all space,
The Cosmic Man, philosopher of grace ;
He found our depth, and touched with tender love
That part of man that lives in form above.

Why fear a loving Father we obey?
What stars afright at God and hide away?
Reciprocation links moon, stars, and sun,
They give and borrow light for every one;
Can Luna hide from Sun who lendeth beams?
She shares her glory with her brightest gleams;
The moon doth love the sun for giving light,
They kiss each other through the longest night;
At morn and eve they meet as laws control,
No fear disturbs, in harmony they roll.

Is faith to intellect what soul's to man?
The soul exists, but not for eyes to scan,
Self-evidence is truth, accepted facts,
The axioms possess what logic lacks;
The one exists, the other mind creates,
Faith grasps the truth while logic still debates;
On wings of faith the angels waft through space,
With power of faith they mount the throne of grace;
With love and faith embrace all facts of right
In trustful faith enjoy all that's delight.

Are solar rays but dawn of future light,
And earth the cradle of a higher flight?
Is babe the germ of knowledge with its force,
To gather wisdom from each cosmic source?
To build the steps to mount the highest tower,
And topple shaft of wrong with giant power,
Or quake a nation with approaching woes,
Subduing tyranny with bloodless blows?
The babe becomes the intellectual form
To sniff the thunder and to kiss the storm.

As endless as the space we occupy,
New facts develop, and so multiply.
Is faith sound evidence of things unseen
Beyond our faculties however keen?
Increasing mental strength, directing powers,
Is evidence unseen as scent of flowers?
Has soul a supplemental, hidden light?
Does faith the higher faculties ignite?
But is it so, my apostolic friend,
My faith was light, on which I still depend?

God's love unbolts the portals to the truth,
I've often felt the sliding bolt from youth ;
God gives the key to knowledge through his laws,
To willing hearts he grants a special clause.
The infinite inspires the finite mind,
And lends us moral strength to search and find ;
As orb in orbit lends poetic time,
And motions of the earth unite in rhyme,
God's power in each dry atom truth displays
Partaking of a force which law obeys.

The seeds of life God gave each scent and kind,
To dimpled child he gives as he designed.
As second's flash reveals expanse of space,
Eternity unveils Jehovah's face ;
A minute's glory how ecstatic, sweet,
When discontent is reconciled complete !
With God and man with faculties ablaze
In glad emotion of His perfect ways,
The God of time is heaven's, too, I know,
The One I love is present, too, below.

In conscious gratitude I rest my case
Upon the rights of man and Jesus' grace ;
My life's an open map before you spread,
You comprehend each thought and word I said ;
Fulfilment of the finite law is past,
The infinite secures a life to last ;
The universe's controlled by wisdom's power,
As true as solar minutes make the hour ;
Obedience is worship, God decreed,
To which he granted grace, all mortals need.

APOSTOLIC SERVANT'S REPLY.

"BUT ye are a chosen generation, a royal priest-hood, a holy nation, a peculiar people ; that ye should show forth the praises of him who hath called you out of darkness into his marvelous light."

"For what glory is it, if, when ye be buffeted for your faults, ye shall take it patiently ? but if, when ye do well, and suffer for it, ye take it patiently, this is acceptable with God." "As free, and not using your liberty for a cloak of maliciousness, but as a servant of God." 1 *Peter 2: 9, 16, 20.*

THE HARBINGER'S WELCOME.

An angel then appeared on scarlet wings
Extending hand, and person'l message brings ;
His face a moral glow with tidings fresh,
But not of human or terrestrial flesh.
He clasped the hand of Lincoln as with power,—
A culminating moment, term'nal hour,—
With words intoned that breathed a welcome call
As Lincoln gazed yet not surprised at all,
Who stood in attitude to meet his guest,
Transfixed in glory that his soul possessed.

The great angelic messenger then spoke,
And these the words that silence softly broke ;
"Upon the edge of pangs I was with thee,
Some psychologic force united me ;
Thy path was ours, thy steps were even mine,
Thy impulse, too, with power that seemed divine ,
Thy hours of slumber mine, to guard and wake,
Thy dreams my thoughts, nor did I thee forsake ;
I was thy hidden staff, thy spirit eyes,
And oft communed without the least surprise.

"Thy mind was yours for me to follow it,
But not to alter acts, or wisdom's wit ;
Thy judgment to confirm and strengthen will,
Encourage heart all duties to fulfil ;
Thy civil and thy military strife —
Profound those mysteries surrounding life.
Upon thy judgment life of millions hung,
And on thy words were stars in ether flung ;
Transporting bliss shall make thy life complete,
A place for thee is wreathed, thy friends to meet.

"Come, mount the steps that lead thee to thy place,
As wide as distance, and as high as space ;
Within the purlieu of still greater things,
Divinity shall send on loving wings ;
The cup of wisdom thou hast filled to brim,
The tree of knowledge climbed to highest limb ;
Thy pillow, truth ; equality, thy rod ;
The path of mercy thou hast always trod ;
Thou 'st freighted moments with thy loving deeds,
And gleaned the best of life 'mong many weeds.

"Thy life no problem but an open page,
Thy work has filled with love a fruitful age ;
Thou 'st plucked the diadem from selfish crown,
And lifted up the poor when trodden down ;
Thou 'st picked the thorns from helpless child of fate,
And opened wide the way and hingeless gate ;
Thou 'st proffered sandals to the feet-sore tramps,
And poured the oil of light into their lamps ;
Thou 'st raised the wounded in thine arms of love,
And kissed the child of sorrow now above.

"To god of wealth thy knees were never bent,
Nor held the toga politicians rent.
Thy eyes were never blurred by truth's clear light,
But sorrow flooded them in silent night.
Thy mirth as clouds of white that float in sky,
That changes scenes while darker clouds pass by ;
Thy solemn gravity the heart oppressed,
As bright enascent thoughts thy moments blessed.
And weight of circumstances never crushed,
For all complaints in bosom slowly hushed.

"He who created elements of earth,
Chaotic night once held in moment's birth,
Assuming orbs, in orbits in their place,
And filling distance of unmeasured space —
Is our Jehovah, Father, and our God,
In whose straight path of wisdom you have trod,
You bent your will toward the goal of right,
And ne'er departed in the darkest night ;
You stood as shaft on island's highest hill,
Unshaken purpose, with determined will.

"From zone to zone thou 'lt pass beyond old time,
Through splendor's zones each growing more sublime,
As intellect develops with each zone,
As we approach still higher, nearing throne ;
Realities thou'lt find beyond thy ken,
As undescribed by words or poet's pen,
Where vastness ocean-like, ne'er overfills,
Yet million streams flow in as mountain rills.
Space widens limitless in rapturous bounds,
As heaven's orchestra through space resounds."

BRIGHT PORTALS OPEN SWUNG.

ABOVE bright zones' horizon, gorgeous hung,
Those portals that in silence open swung,
Where busy angels holy welcome bowed,
As voices raised their tunes exulting loud.
With gravity he mounts the beryl step,
As measured rhythmic time the voices kept,
Within the corridor of heaven's grace,
Who met the cherubim with radiant face,
Where principalities in order reign,
And human virtues first promotion gain.

COMMENTS.

Your comments write beneath this soaring bird,
With his majestic freedom in each word.

PRESENTED

REMARKS.

As independent as the owl on guard,
Pen your remarks, philosopher or bard.

THE PRIME HERO

THE PRIME HERO.

INSCRUTABLE, occult, the power of God,
Whose law dissolves each formed Adamic clod,
Who honors characters of truth, and " sweat,"
And every burning thought that minds beget.
Each soul shall reap the harvest of its deeds,
While rev'ling microbes on its body feeds.
Grand law of life the microbe must obey;
As rose organic life to bloom a day,
So nations must obey organic law,
Or see the clash of arms our people saw.

The flame of "none extension" lit the hour
Which agitation fed; combustive power,
Upon the altar Douglas did erect,
To slavery uphold or to reject.
He then as flaming giant from the sky
Threw bolts of logic with a gunner's eye ;
Old Mason-Dixon line he broke as thread,
While Lincoln's voice for "none extension" plead ;
(The admiration of unfettered free,
Emerging coral shaft from troubled sea).

His pulse in unison with people's beat,
Unchanged by storm, and never raised by heat,
Nor exaltation altered man of fate,
With all the force of war and power of state;
The rights of man unknown to king or knave,
A jewel in each crown that Lincoln gave;
No other age evolved just such as he,
Nor was intensified to such degree;
He brushed away a cloud as with a fan,
The God who lit the sun gave us the man.

On sun-kissed promontory Lincoln stood,
Premonitor of right for nation'l good;
To move to either side strange peril yawned,
While restless Notus blew where hazard dawned;
The world was gazing on transcending man,
Through every party lens the hero scan;
While taking Washington's untarnished chair,
The people's will selecting him the heir;
Just fresh from western sunset's glowing rim,
With all the courage that belonged to him.

His life was not the pebbled, purling brook,
Nor lazy worm's that gnaws the miser's book ;
Each pulse that gave him life was all he had,
When changing childhood to the busy lad ;
He sought each printed line which opened mind,
To watch his thoughts, to learn how they 're inclined ;
The impulse of his heart he learned was right,
As purity was pleasure and delight ;
The Master's teaching guided early course,
Which grew in power as he developed force.

To build a star none but a God could do,
A body made of light and atoms new—
To twinkle in its orbit distant sun —
Yet light a universe of orbs, as one ;
The God of stars a child from matter hurled—
Igniting soul with force to light a world !
Of rarest force inherent powers sustain,
From bone to flesh, to nerve and peerless brain ;
Uncouth foundation, superstructure grand —
The God of stars had built as he had planned.

The child, the lad, and youth's maturing man,
The higher force exhibits in his plan.
Design was hid in cradle of the babe,
That forced to agile, athlete, wrestling "Abe,"
Then axman, soldier, up to legal sprig,
Conviction molded into loyal Whig ;
His hand and brain together using time,
To build a character to grow sublime ;
From ashes of the hearth first ate his bread,
And stars first spangled cover, leaves his bed.

The bitter weeds the autumn fires scorch,
He gathered into fagots for a torch,
By which he read his books and studied law,
Increasing blaze when autumn nights were raw.
Ambition never blushed in gath'ring facts,
Nor fresh embarrassment could check his acts ;
No trail so tortuous he could not keep,
No barrier too high for him to leap,
No laws so intricate he could not solve,
No injury so great to not absolve.

The rose, with wealth no other blooms possess,
Yet grows on thorns, none love the scent the less ,
When tasseled corn from moisture droughts deprive,
The force of want makes roots the deeper drive ;
Our Hero lived in want, but not for brains,
Tho' cabin born, he soon was handling reins ;
The treeless plains inspiring campus walk,
Who soared above the college like a hawk ;
With latent strength he pounced upon the truth,
Each moment forging history from youth.

None but a child of poverty can feel
The force of want, when hunger makes appeal ;
None but the coatless child can ever know
The weight of crystal flakes of drifting snow ;
None but a heart once crushed to deep despair,
Can soothe another's heart with gentle care.
Those lessons Lincoln learned to not forget,
Applying each as circumstances met,
As master of himself each to employ,
To mold philosopher of plastic boy.

"A man of many sides" as carbon stone,
A crystal gem from every side has shown,
And cut and polished by the art of peace,
In rayless night must brilliancy increase.
"A man of many sides," and each was bright,
While slow in growth he reached his normal height ;
To grasp imperial power, yet be uncrowned,
In every crisis for the right was found ;
Who seemed to follow, but had always led,
And used the bellows 'til his steel was red.

Once architect and master of a boat,
As graceful swan on rippling waters float ;
As captain of his craft, he "loaded" low,
The river current moved impatient, slow.
He winds his way to Orleans' cloudy south,
That nestles near the Mississippi's mouth ;
There slavery in all its phases saw —
Amalgamation, whip, and block, and law —
A picture stamped upon his youthful heart,
High destiny had fixed as guiding chart.

Immeasurable depth of moral power,
With psychologic force, as scent in flower,
And self-volition's cultured brain combined,
Uniting all, produced majestic mind.
His idiosyncrasies he understood,
The higher knowledge daily mental food,
'Til smothered heat of deep volcano burst,
To spend exhaustless power on Douglas first.
He measured self in judgment, he the judge,
Who knew himself no fallacy could budge.

Now peer met peer on forum of debate,
On Squatter-Sovereignty, creating state ;
Antagonistic minds as strong as bold,
Ambitious statesmen's sentiments to mold.
As distant thunder Douglas hurling thought,
Reverberating space his meaning caught.
Then Lincoln raised his voice, extending arms,
Whose oratory people quickly charms,
"A house divided cannot stand!" exclaimed,
Congested politics at once inflamed.

Those words were gladiator's fearless blow,
Their vibratory power no one can know.
At Appomattox they were clearly heard,
Capitulating sword to Lincoln's word ;
That sentence moved a Nation's martial heart,
With clash of arms that follow as a part ;
The house divided, but it could not fall,
Its deep foundation held the solid wall ;
That house remains the temple of the brave,
On which the stars and stripes shall ever wave.

Those words are products of that fruitful Tree,
That beareth fruit of which is always free.
The words pronounced by Lincoln, sacred speech,
As Master's saying, still that lesson teach ;
No words were ever spoken freighted more
With truth and power in gospel sacred lore ;
Life's unity our Master had in view,
And Lincoln used expression aptly too.
Applied to country undivided one,
And indivisible as orb of sun.

Accomplished orators portend the storm,
Then gathering combustion into form,
They saw cold chivalry and justice clash,
And distant thunders coming with a crash ;
As Douglas firm, and Lincoln solemn, spoke,
The Nation from its lethargy awoke ;
State conflict was approaching, they declared,
Of ghostly form, in darkness danger glared,
Who drove their logic as unbridled steeds,
To tragic field of gore where justice pleads.

To retrospect through vista's gauzy veil,
Investigating birth must doubtless fail ;
Why one's a hero born, the other, slave,
Some born to wreck the Nation, some to save,
Are problems embryology still seals,
Where life and soul unite and form reveals.
Our hero came as must the dwarf in mode,
All travel lifehood's enigmatic road ;
The hero as the mountain towering high,
Pale dwarf is cradled as a toy to die.

The combination of his soul and mind
In equipoise divinity designed ;
He kissed the smiling babe with dirty face,
As image of its God, with simple grace ;
'T was not the ruffled nor the satin dressed
That he embraced or to his bosom pressed ;
'T was not the garb of man first to admire,
Nor distant ancestry or hero sire ;
'T was man and only man, full-measured man,
That he respected, or the future can.

He was a man, no more ; but nobly such,
With principle that ne'er required a crutch.
A mind so organized with inner light,
Applying reason with augmented sight.
With active thinking power, and oft acute,
When analyzing things in warm dispute,
His thinking cells were multiplied so great,
Increased capacity with strength and weight.
Wild seed he never planted, life to drain,
Nor withered by debauch a fertile brain.

He had a seer's directness of his own
In solving acts, and then missteps condone;
A subtle power inspired by highest good,
Whose spirit-intellect best understood,
Between the known, and intuition saw,
The shadow first, and then the perfect law;
In transit measured thought as science gale,
Or zephyrs change to storm and drop to hail;
His apt conclusions axiomatic strong,
For logic was his antidote for wrong.

Who would expunge the conflict of this age,
While Nation'l glory flames from every page?
Who dullen memory of civil war,
With all that Christian goodness must abhor?
As well deface the country's latest map,
And empty tropic gulf in polar lap,
Deorbit zenith sun, his spots to hide,
As try to rob the Union of its pride;
The North and South, together make a whole,
Both equal dear that filled a Lincoln's soul.

What splendor centered in our Hero's court,
Where wealth could fawn and politicians sport,
And military stars their brightness shone,
And great ambassadors from regal throne,
And admirals who oil the waves to sleep,
And men who weigh the microbe of the deep,
And scientist with gun of heatless fire,—
All gather'd round the court him to admire,
And gazed in wonderment at Lincoln's form,
The living center of the civil storm.

To paint him less, the power that heaven gave,
Would be as painting ocean, less the wave;
To paint him with the latent force he had,
In meditative mood sublimely sad,
Would be as painting iridescent bow,
That spans eternal fields of crystal snow;
The echoes of his deeds no limit bounds,
And every race of men his praise resounds,
Is evidence of wisdom few possessed,
Who rode ambition's tide on highest crest.

His enigmatic mirth as rippling rill ;
Tho' deeper life in thought provoking still,
Yet solemn gravity showed wit as bright,
As phosphorescent flash of sea-born light ;
The ostentatious ridiculed with wit,
With garnishment a dude unblushing "hit."
His jokes were parabolical in style,
With storming laughter, followed with a smile.
His jests as spiral spring, give either way,
With facial muscles fixed to change or stay.

He penetrated light with mental eyes,
As eagle sun intensity defies,
Spontaneous wit in him as sparks ignite,
Withal judicial mind who grasped the right.
He weighs the proposition in his mind,
With strange alacrity solutions find ;
His magnanimity hard knots unloosed,
The man unmeasured, Liberty produced ;
The child of poverty met death in power,
As martyr of his faith's exalted hour.

Sweet lyre of motherhood, by cherubs strung,
You welcome new-born child with harp and song.
Pure shrine of mother, loving thoughts attend,
As seer and hero in devotion bend ;
The gates of heaven swing upon thy law,
The acme of sublimity and awe !
Hope's incarnation, mother's natal love,
It comes from God, and must return above.
A cabin child, still halo's Nancy Hanks,
To her a nation bows eternal thanks.

His rising manhood gazed o'er prairie plains,
Horizon limits rugged growth explains.
His hungry mind absorbed with glowing heart,
Rich nature's fullest strength, with help of art.
Intensifying thought, igniting will,
Expanding mental organs with a thrill ;
Developing the brain to pond'rous weight,
Dilating heart to ethics high estate,
His own curriculum conferred degrees,
By larded torch, with book upon his knees.

Our hero slowly grew, perchance as stars ;
Time's cycles gave us scintillating Mars.
His early mind was no precocious blaze,
Exhausted quick, but grew as summer days.
His brain receptacle as fountain well,
Life's hopes as mountain-peaks that never fell ;
With love as thermal space around the sun,
And courage that the world's applause has won.
Not faultless though,—perfection is divine,—
Yet name of " Honest Abe," could not decline.

His narrow path of private life was clean,
No filth or garbage in that path was seen,
As open as the sun's the world to see,
And trod his daily rounds twixt law and plea.
Oft looked upon his narrow limit rounds,
To wonder what should be his future bounds ;
As failure in a mask upon him gazed,
But still his purpose as a beacon blazed,
He felt his boundaries extending slight —
Defeat the torch that lit him to his height.

So when the chariot came, clean was the way,
No mud to splash, or boulders to delay.
His mind and heart were ready for the change,
So full of truth that nothing true was strange.
Political philosophy as plain
As were the steps he took to purpose gain ;
The public heart he understood was true,
The people's will was his, to theirs pursue.
The Hero saw and felt as duty bid,
No motive gilded nor defect was hid.

Since person'l rights and liberty were born,
No other man did freedom more adorn ;
With power as limitless as sovereign might,
Without abusing one inherent right,
To honor every claim his honest pride,
And none the weight of truth he e'er denied ;
Whose word could stay an army corps from death,
As life of thousands trembled on his breath.
Yet ready mercy hovered on each word,
As throbbing heart of love was ever heard.

What blood and energy the conflict cost.
To weigh the gain, subtracting what was lost,
Philosophers may solve in fruitful time,
Computing good, and then deducting crime ;
The art of war proficiency enhanced,
On land and ocean sciences advanced ;
Neglected forces were aroused from dreams,
Realities were cast from drossy themes ;
Like dead volcanoes with new fire and smoke,
From lake to gulf new energy awoke.

Now peaceful victory of heart and brain,
Like subterraneous streams appear again,
And bubbling in their laughter full of mirth,
With growth of commerce and the fruits of earth ;
O'er fields of war the eagle proudly flies,
And monuments of honor now arise.
The rose and lily bent o'er Blue and Gray,
The night of gloom developed into day,
With all the rays of solar force and heat,
In every part the union is complete.

While ocean waves shall dash on rock-bound coast,
We 'll guard our land with freedom's gallant host ;
Our mountains send their men without request,
And valley rush to arms, selecting best.
When prairies gather force as autumn fires,
And sons of youthful years shall follow sires,
Whose shouts of "Union!" echoes never hush,
Nor enemy their native valor crush ;
When mothers charge their boys to meet the foe,
As North and South together strike the blow.

If every cloud that floats in freedom's arch,
That breaks the summer heat, assuaging parch,
And every lunar change, bestowing light,
That spreads her beams on virtue's path of night,
And every planet dart that reaches earth,
Each adding some new truth to freedom's worth,
Must culminate, rekindling Lincoln's name,
Who never faltered from determined aim,
But like the Mississippi's constant flow,
Augmenting force continued still to grow.

Denude the mountains of their granite domes,
Remove the purest marble white as Rome's,
Prepare a base of granite, hardest grit,
Erect a shaft as high as clouds permit,
Cementing base with flux of silver pure,
Ornating joints and bolt with steel secure ;
With iron crane lay cubes on solid base,
In golden flux, each one in proper place ;
What feeble grandeur, yet superb in plan,
To show the majesty of such a man !

Go back through labyrinth of brooding time, [crime ;
When kings enjoyed their place through blood and
Imperial power divine, through birth and state,
When royalty meant power and power its weight ;
To see their coffer brimming with their spoils,
Still wet from tears, and red from servile toils ;
Return to love a heart as Lincoln had,
The cabin child, and poverty's brave lad,
To see the crowning power of earthly things,
Unshackled intellect on angel wings.

STANDING BY HIS CATAFALQUE.

I STOOD beside that marbled Hero's bier,
Upon the floor he stood when he was here;
Where oft his eloquence took soaring flights,
While advocating truth and human rights.
I bowed my head awe-bent, but not to weep,
But let my mind revolve while he's asleep;
To meditate upon the martyred dead,
Who served his age for which his blood was shed;
As deeds now penetrate, beyond to reach,
Results of tragic death mock words of speech.

I looked upon that alabaster face,
Whose living lines of character I trace,
As when I saw him sixty months before,
That tall, athletic man upon this floor,
Just ready for the task the people gave
The civil hero yet in danger brave;
No mark of anguish left on pond'rous brow,
Nor furrow changed by time's all-turning plow;
While lips are sealed to me, to God they're not,
Nor is the foul conspiracy and plot.

What massive head! an empire was his brain,
No human weight that he could not sustain ;
No human pain but he could learn to bear,
No human grief that caused him to despair ;
No disappointment changed his normal course,
Nor war nor peace affecting mental force ;
His multiplied resources never dried,
As scientific knowledge he applied.
Who had a splint for every broken plan,
And never looked above the common man.

And still I gazed upon that rugged face,
In meditation lost, and to the place !
I tried to penetrate those bony walls,
To gather in my mind what most appalls ;
The laceration of his soul's domains,
God's grandest mechanism,— thinking brains
Where spirit life and intellectu'l powers,
Unite to cluster as the fragrant flowers ;
So intricate that seraphim would blush
To change a fiber, or a cell to crush.

Now cold the hand that penned the great decree
To make the man of natal pigments free.
The culminating glory of his soul,
Immortal he who wrote unblotted scroll.
Cold hand, cold arm of giant strength are numb,
The nimble finger, and the ready thumb
Are motionless — are dead, yes ! dead are they —
To dust return, transmuted into clay !
Should atom as a spark transmission claim,
It might ignite another living flame.

But still I gazed as oft in life I had,
With mind absorbed and heart inverted sad,
To wonder why a noble life should end,
Within a throng, and all but one a friend.
Then came a whisper as from other shore,
"His course was finished,— he could do no more,"
The sun may oft intensify a ray,
But can't increase his limits of a day ;
The fulness of his time for purpose came,
His work completed, God himself to claim.

PANEGYRIC.

The solar orb may drop his carbon stone,
To stud imperial crown upon the throne,
Hot comets fling their molten gold on earth,
What mote as circumstance compared to birth?
Where child immortal forces shall enhance —
While virtue spurs ambition to advance ;
And sacred cabin of the pioneers,
Sweet nurseries of past, the present cheers,
Imprinting pious truth on crystal mind,
Procrastination gave to lead mankind.

Our Hero chiseled as from living rock,
The child of freedom from a flawless block,
Who grew to upright man the people thrilled,
With fervent heart that height had never chilled ;
Those qualities which make a loving man,
Through arteries and veins as quickened ran.
No person'l myth or Oriental Jove
Who flaming steeds through fiery distance drove ;
He was the living Alpha to the end,
Omega in his place as people's friend.

In magnitude he rose beyond the great,
Whose known diameter involved but state ;
His ocean bound, and held in strong embrace,
Protecting each, and still extending space ;
Our crystal age affords but one of such,
Whose harmony was felt at every touch.
One Lincoln in a century's enough,
To rob creation of such vital stuff ;
Another age may need perchance some more,
The growth of Liberty on our shore.

He knew no section in his march with time,
No politics but factors that were prime ;
One country his, of equal rights in plan,
One destiny of elevated man,
One dignity to toiler of the spade,
With him who millions honestly has made ;
One honor to the bayonet and sword,
Who render love to Him whom he adored.
Capacious heart, the larger, loving kind,
No party limits bound his lib'ral mind

Exalted man in health of matchless life,
The moment slew beside a loving wife,
Who passed from flesh as gleam from heaven's cloud,
As missile through the cerebellum plowed,
The limpéd body robbed of life and mind,
Upon the lap of woe in death reclined.
And mourning millions bend o'er casket lid,
Whose soul the weeping angels welcome bid ;
Like shining star in distant ether crushed,
To higher zone of space ignition rushed !

Intelligence was dumb — unconscious lies —
Immortal President a martyr dies ;
All potency of life betokens grief,
And irrepressible hearts throb, for chief !
The lily and the rose sad, stricken, bent,
As tears in dew and mist upon them sent.
Sun rays that passed through distant, starless space,
Each, iridescent, dipped to kiss his face ;
Such splendor, mellowed light of sorrows tell,
Subdued as accents that from lips then fell.

The mountains seemed to rock, and valleys rise,
And flow of rivers move with self-surprise,
The ocean tide-lashed foam was piled on shore,
As birds in groups were chirping in their lore.
The rising sun was fire, no rays to shed,
And mounts the sky reluctant flaming red ;
Men's eyes were staring balls, in pallid face ;
For century was blotted with disgrace.
The daring blow at freedom touched each soul,
As mournful thunders through the heavens roll.

Our conquered liberty's embalmed in him,
Whose golden chalice death has filled to brim,
His risen star, the molded wrongs of past,
Faith, liberty, and death in orbit cast ;
In coming ages still augmenting light,
And every ray intensifying right,
'Til truth reflects equality of man,
Upon the "Meek and Lowly's" simple plan ;
Then strikes shall cease, and destitution too,
And all shall right and honesty pursue.

He stands on heaven's battlement, just where
Horizon meets horizon's neutral air,
Beyond time's zone in heaven's vital space,
To plead the cause of every cognate race.
As columns of unmeasured depth appear,
With hopes eternal in the soul to cheer.
His work the object of celestial care,
Whose efforts never cease his joy to share,
This side the sacred limits of the throne,
Eternity's no place for spirit drone.

Let mind review a retrospect of man ;
Five thousand years of progress let us scan.
Each noble man of history profane,
And study character and measure brain ;
Then weigh the heart on scales of perfect poise,
The age and times, the light that oft decoys ;
Count pyramids and monuments as planned,
The shafts of wonder still to glory stand ;
Who has approached his altitude on earth,
Through force of manhood, freedom's highest worth ?

When time has spent its force to be no more,
Consuming ocean's chasm recedes from shore,
Hot mountains crumble, filling yawning place,
And deep'ning craters flame in lurid space.
When calm approaches, matter disappears,
And heaven's convoy distant music hears,
Then open wide shall swing celestial gate,
Where seraph's concourse welcome bidding wait,
In midst of gate the hero comes in sight,
While human hosts with angels there unite.